MAIDSTONE

20.   09

1 8 AUG 2

C153645834

EXTREME

Defying
Gravity

Surviving Extreme Sports

Sean Callery

A & C Black • London

WARNING!
Defying gravity can be deadly dangerous. Never try any of the things you see in this book without the help of a qualified instructor.

KENT
LIBRARIES & ARCHIVES
C153645834

Produced for A & C Black by
MONKEY PUZZLE MEDIA LTD
Monkey Puzzle Media Ltd
The Rectory, Eyke, Woodbridge
Suffolk IP12 2QW, UK

Published by A & C Black Publishers Limited
38 Soho Square, London W1D 3HB

First published 2008
Copyright © 2008 A & C Black Publishers Limited

ISBN 978-1-4081-0026-4 (hardback)
ISBN 978-1-4081-0092-9 (paperback)

All rights reserved. No part of this publication may be reproduced, stored in a retrieval system or transmitted in any form, electronic, mechanical, photocopying, recording or otherwise, without prior permission of A & C Black Publishers Limited.

The right of Sean Callery to be identified as the author of this Work has been asserted by him in accordance with the Copyright, Designs and Patents Act 1988.

A CIP catalogue record for this book is available from the British Library.

Editor: Polly Goodman
Design: Mayer Media Ltd
Picture research: Lynda Lines
Series consultant: Jane Turner

This book is produced using paper that is made from wood grown in managed, sustainable forests. It is natural, renewable and recyclable. The logging and manufacturing processes conform to the environmental regulations of the country of origin.

Printed in China by C & C Offset Printing Co., Ltd

Picture acknowledgements
Action Plus pp. 6 (Richard Francis), 7 (Michel Pissotte), 9 (Andy Day), 11 (Tony Donaldson), 19 (Steve Bardens); Alamy pp. 1 (Adrian Sherratt), 10 (Buzz Pictures), 22 (Adrian Sherratt), 26 (Chris A Crumley); Corbis pp. 8 (Louis Moses), 15 (Ted Levine/Zefa), 24 (Michael Kevin Daly), 25 (David Madison); Getty Images pp. 4 (Randy Lincks), 5 (AFP), 14 (PatitucciPhoto), 17 (AFP), 18, 21, 28 (Peter Sterling), 29 (Norbert Eisele-Hein); iStockphoto p. 16 (Jason Lugo); Will Linford pp. 12–13; Photolibrary.com p. 20 (Valerie Mathilde/Images du Sud); Rex Features pp. 23 (Stewart Cook), 27 (Zena Holloway).

The front cover shows a snowboarder in the air (Alamy/Stock Connection).

Every effort has been made to contact copyright holders of material reproduced in this book. Any omissions will be rectified in subsequent printings if notice is given to the publishers.

CONTENTS

Abbreviations m stands for metres • **ft** stands for feet • **in** stands for inches •
km stands for kilometres • **km/h** stands for kilometres per hour • **mph** stands for miles per hour

Would you fall for it?

Aiee!

Would you trust your life to the strength of an elastic band? That's what bungee jumpers do when they leap from high bridges, platforms and even hot-air balloons or helicopters, and plummet towards the ground.

Just as they are about to hit the ground, elastic cords stop their fall and pull them back up into the air. After a few more falls and bounces, the jumpers hang around to be rescued.

Helicopter plunge

The longest ever bungee jump was made by stuntman Dave Barlia, in June 2001. He dropped 1,800 metres (6,000 feet) from a helicopter over California's Mohave Desert before the bungee cord hauled him back. The unstretched cord was 550 metres (1,800 feet) long.

Gravity pulls the jumper down until the cord has stretched as far as it can.

gravity the force pulling everything towards the Earth

Boing!
The upwards **force** of the cord bouncing back is stronger than gravity, so the jumper is pulled up.

UPWARDS FORCE

Whoa!

The cord is made from many strands of stretchy rubber.

The length of the cord depends on the weight of the jumper. Heavy people have shorter cords because their weight pulls them down more.

GRAVITY

force a push or a pull that makes things slow down, speed up, or change shape

What a drag

Skydivers have plenty of time to admire the view as they fall. Many skydivers say they feel as if they are floating, not falling.

GRAVITY

Spreading the arms and legs increases the **air resistance** and slows the fall.

AIR RESISTANCE

air resistance the force of air pushing against a moving object

Wing suits

Some skydiving suits have webbing under the arms and between the legs that acts like wings. These suits allow the diver to fly sideways (horizontally) as well as down (vertically).

*Skydivers who fall head first in a **streamlined** shape can reach speeds of 320 km/h (200 mph) because the air resistance is reduced.*

The air makes a roaring sound as it rushes past the skydiver, pushing up against gravity and resisting the skydiver's fall. At first, skydivers fall faster and faster, but after 15 seconds the air resistance equals the force of gravity and they reach a constant speed of about 200 kilometres per hour (124 miles per hour). This is called terminal velocity.

streamlined   with a smooth shape that can move quickly through air or water

City gyms

The city is a giant obstacle course for free runners. They leap between rooftops, somersault from walls and vault over barriers in a Superman-like display through the city streets.

Free runners put one or both hands on top of a wall or railings and swing their legs up to propel themselves over.

Superman roll

In this move, free runners jump with their arms outstretched into a forward roll, tucking their heads under and rolling on to their back before standing up and continuing forwards.

vault   to leap using the hands or a pole

Sometimes gravity is the free runner's friend, pulling the runners down for a safe landing. At other times they fight it, pushing off from a firm foothold to leap up and forwards. When the energy of the jump runs out, gravity brings them down.

In a movement called the tic tac, the runner plants one or both feet on a vertical obstacle such as a wall and pushes on from it.

UPWARDS FORCE

FORWARD MOVEMENT

GRAVITY

Lying low

What zooms along roads at wheel-melting speeds and only 5 centimetres (2 inches) above the ground? A street luger! For these street racers, speed is everything – no tricks allowed.

Street luge boards are long enough for the riders to lie down on their back, feet outstretched in front. The lugers race each other on downhill courses through sealed-off city streets. After a starting push, the riders lie as low on the board as possible, just off the ground.

Holy smoke! A street luger tries desperately to slow down at the end of the course.

Hot feet!

The only brakes are the lugers' shoes, which they drag along the ground to create **friction** and slow down. Some lugers attach chunks of car tyre to their shoes so they don't wear out so quickly.

friction   a force between two touching objects that opposes movement

A leather body suit streamlines the rider's shape and reduces air resistance.

AIR RESISTANCE

GRAVITY

Gravity pulls the board down the slope.

Roll with it

Skateboarding is one of the most popular individual sports in the world. This is because you can do it on any hard surface, and there are lots of tricks and jumps to perform.

The ollie is a no-hands jump in which the skater "pops" the board into the air by tapping the tail on the ground. Here's how it's done.

2 Straighten legs and raise arms to generate upward force.

DOWNWARDS FORCE

UPWARDS FORCE

1 Crouch low with back foot on the tail of the board.

3 Push the back foot down to raise the front of the board.

4 Board **pivots** around back wheels.

pivot to turn around something

The most important move in skateboarding is the ollie. This move is the starting point for most **aerial** tricks because of the way it defies gravity. Then there's the frontside 180, a **half-pipe** move where the skater performs a mid-air turn and seems to hang in the air as they twist, returning to the ramp facing the opposite way.

The ollie

The ollie is named after its creator, Alan "Ollie" Gelfand, who invented it in 1978. (Ollie was his nickname.)

Flat shoes increase the friction between the feet and the board, for better grip.

GRAVITY

6 Bend knees to cushion the impact on landing.

FORWARD MOVEMENT

5 Slide front foot forwards to drag the board forwards. This also rotates the board to make it level.

Gravity words

Vertical, or "vert" skating is skateboarding with "big air" jumps, often on a half-pipe in a skateboard park. Deck is another name for the flat surface of the skateboard.

aerial in the air   **half-pipe** a U-shaped ramp used in extreme sports

Rock steady

Uh oh!

Bouldering is like a game of chess – climbers have to think their way around a "problem", as the rocky obstacles are known. If they get it wrong, they fall.

Boulderers don't want to climb up high. Their main aim is to put together a series of movements to get past tricky rock formations, including overhangs. Then they pick their way through, using friction to cling to the rocks like Spider-Man. Boulderers only climb up to about 3–5 metres (10–16 feet) above the ground, but even a fall of that distance is scary and dangerous.

A thick, foam crash mat is left on the ground beneath the climbers to absorb the impact if they fall.

Chalky powder keeps sweaty fingers and palms dry. This increases the friction and grip between the fingers and the rock.

Toes jam into narrow cracks.

Rock climbing shoes have soft rubber soles for maximum grip.

Powder power

Snowboarding is a bit like skateboarding on snow, but much faster. The highest speed reached on a snowboard was nearly 202 kilometres per hour (126 miles per hour) in 1999.

Slalom snowboarders race downhill at teeth-juddering pace, carving through the snow as they zigzag between the **slalom** gates (poles). Others go freestyle from the half-pipe, soaring up from the ramp to defy gravity with "big air" tricks, flips and jumps.

In this aerial trick, called a frontside grab, the snowboarder holds the board and changes direction.

slalom a race over a zigzag course between markers

Goofy or regular?

Snowboarders who ride with their left foot forwards have "regular" feet. Those who ride with their right foot forwards are said to have "goofy" feet.

Steel edges dig into the snow to make turning easier.

The friction between the board and the snow melts a thin layer of ice. This **lubricates** the board and makes it slide faster.

To turn, the snowboarder puts more weight on the front foot and leans into the turn, tilting on to the toes or heels depending on the direction of the turn.

Wax lubricates the bottom of the board and makes it faster.

lubricate to add something to reduce friction

Shock value

Zooming down a hill on a bike is a real buzz. Mountain bikers do it while dodging rocks and streams at eye-watering speed. Oh, and some are racing against the clock.

Downhill mountain bikers can easily reach 100 kilometres per hour (60 miles per hour) as they hurtle down steep hills, so their bikes need really powerful brakes. The bikes also have to be sturdy enough to survive the punishing jolts and bumps.

Riders haul on the rear brake to skid around corners. But if they pull too much the back wheel will skid out from underneath the rider.

Suspension

Shock absorbers on mountain bikes are called suspension. They allow the wheel to travel up and down by about 15 centimetres (6 inches) to absorb the bumps, so the rider doesn't get bounced around as much.

shock absorbers   equipment that reduces the impact of sudden movement

The rider keeps his weight over the rear wheel by crouching behind the saddle. This helps the rear wheel to grip.

The front brake provides most of the stopping power so it is used much more than the rear brake.

Tyres are **wide** and have a **knobbly** texture for maximum friction and grip.

Shock absorbers cushion the impact from uneven ground.

FRICTION

The rail way

How does an in-line skater get down a set of steps? Never mind "hold the hand rail" – they jump on to it and "grind" down!

Aggressive in-line skaters grind or slide along anything in their way. Their four- or five-wheel skates allow them to perform tricks on the street or from half-pipes in skateboard parks. The skates have a plastic or steel **grind plate** fitted next to the wheels for sliding down rails and other obstacles – a move that would shred the wheels of skates for general riding.

In-line skates for general riding have big, soft wheels and a brake pad at the back. The wheels have better friction and grip than the smaller wheels on aggressive in-line skates.

Gravity words

To "grind" in aggressive in-line skating is to slide down an obstacle using the grind plates on the sides of the skates. Tricks are difficult movements.

grind plate   a length of hard plastic or steel that protects the wheels when sliding down obstacle

The "unity" trick is a grind with legs crossed, sliding on the outside edge of each skate.

The skate's hard edge **slides** down the rail.

Small, hard wheels don't get in the way of tricks, like larger wheels.

SCREEEEECH!

FRICTION

Free wheels

Dirtboards are a cross between a skateboard and a snowboard, but their large wheels mean they don't have to wait for snow and they can handle dirt and grass, so they're free to hurtle around in more places.

Dirtboarding is especially popular in ski resorts when the snow has melted. Freeriders weave between the poles of the downhill slalom, crossing their opponents' paths to put them off. Freestylers head for the ramp to show off dizzying multiple spins, flips and grabs.

Now that's big air! Dirtboarders do similar aerial tricks to skateboarders.

Gravity words

Dirtboarding is also known as all-terrain boarding, mountain boarding, landboarding and grassboarding.

pneumatic filled with air

Outstretched arms keep the rider balanced.

Leaning forwards helps gravity pull the rider down the hill.

Soft, **pneumatic** tyres absorb impact.

Leaning sideways shifts the rider's balance and helps him turn.

The rider's feet are attached to the board with bindings to increase their grip.

balance   an even distribution of weight that allows someone to stay upright and not fall over

23

Riding the rapids

Whitewater rafting pits people against one of the most dangerous forces of nature: fast-flowing water. A light, inflatable boat is swept along by a river's current while its passengers steer between rocks.

The water in a river is pulled downhill towards the sea by gravity. This creates the current, which can get incredibly strong when the river flows through narrow gaps or down steep inclines. Areas of fast-flowing, shallow water are known as rapids, and they give the boat a rough ride.

Whitewater rafters hold on tight as they drop down an incline.

CURRENT

Gravity pulls water and boat downhill.

inflatable filled with air

Light on water

Whitewater rafts are heavy on land but light and easy to move on water. This is because the **upthrust** from the water reduces the effect of gravity.

GRAVITY

CURRENT

UPTHRUST

Water pushes up against the bottom of the raft giving it upthrust.

upthrust   upward force when an object is in a liquid

How low can you go?

How long can you hold your breath for? How long could you hold it while diving down into the ocean, knowing that you've got to have enough oxygen in your lungs to make it back to the surface?

This is freediving, where divers swim as deep as they can without an oxygen supply. Gravity pulls them down, but upthrust pushes them up. Freedivers form a streamlined shape to fight against this upward force as they power their way down into the dark depths.

Divers must come to the surface slowly or they risk pain, and even death, from the change in water pressure.

Record dive

The current freedive record is a dive that lasted 3 minutes and 28 seconds and reached 83 metres (270 feet).

oxygen   the gas we need to breathe

26

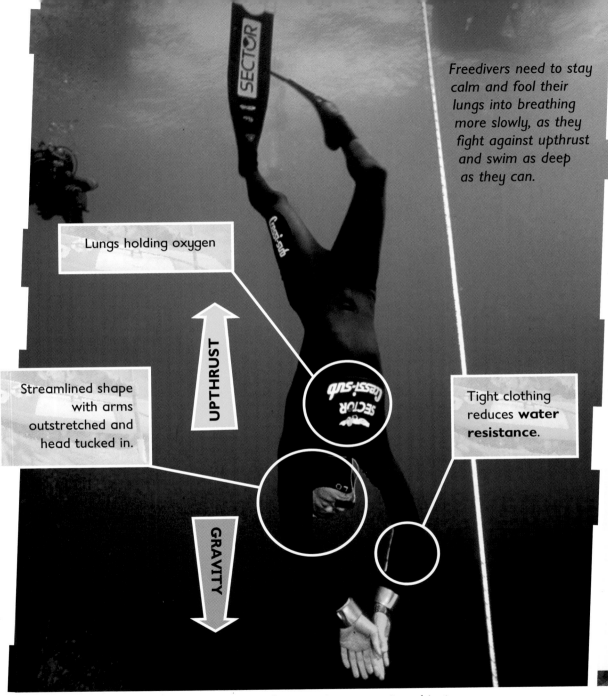

Freedivers need to stay calm and fool their lungs into breathing more slowly, as they fight against upthrust and swim as deep as they can.

Lungs holding oxygen

UPTHRUST

Streamlined shape with arms outstretched and head tucked in.

Tight clothing reduces **water resistance**.

GRAVITY

water resistance   the force of water pushing against a moving object

Give us a wave

Kitesurfing takes surfing to a new level by allowing the surfer to take off into the air and perform tricks above the waves.

Kitesurfing boards are much smaller than surfboards. Footstraps stop surfers losing their board as they soar into the air. A harness attaches the surfer to a power kite, designed to catch every whisper of wind.

The kite can be used as a sail to create a forward force that pulls the board and rider across the water.

Ocean riding

In May 2006, French kitesurfer Manu Bertin crossed the Atlantic Ocean in a three-week ride of 5,600 kilometres (3,480 miles). He used three different types of board, including an inflatable boat in which he could rest and eat.

The kite (or sail) lifts the surfer out of the water.

LIFT

Kite lines

The harness is attached to the kite lines, which are pulled by the kite.

GRAVITY

The wind in the kite creates an upwards force that is bigger than gravity and pulls the surfer away from the water.

Glossary

aerial in the air

air resistance the force of air pushing against a moving object

balance an even distribution of weight that allows someone to stay upright and not fall over

force a push or a pull that makes things slow down, speed up, or change shape

friction a force between two touching objects that opposes movement

gravity the force pulling everything towards the Earth

grind plate a length of hard plastic or steel that protects the wheels of an inline skate when sliding down obstacles

half-pipe a U-shaped ramp used in extreme sports, such as skateboarding, in-line skating and snowboarding

inflatable filled with air

lubricate to add something to reduce friction

oxygen the gas we need to breathe

pivot to turn around something

pneumatic filled with air

shock absorbers equipment that reduces the impact of sudden movement

slalom a race over a zigzag course between markers

streamlined with a smooth shape that can move quickly through air or water

upthrust upward force when an object is in a liquid

vault to leap using the hands or a pole

water resistance the force of water pushing against a moving object

Further information

Books

Extreme Sports
(DK Readers: Level 3) by
Richard Platt (Dorling
Kindersley, 2001)
Accounts of some extreme
sports told in story form.

Extreme Sports by Joe
Tomlinson (Carlton, 2004)
An encyclopedia of extreme
sports giving their history,
important figures, and
techniques.

**Extreme Sports – No
Limits** (Crabtree, 2004)
A series covering different
sports, including profiles of
the big names.

Extreme Sports Stars
by Philip Abraham
(Scholastic, 2007)
Profiles of the top names in
various extreme sports.

No Limits (Franklin Watts,
2005)
A series of books giving the
lowdown on a range of
extreme sports by title.

Films

Casino Royale directed by
Martin Campbell (MGM,
2006; Certificate 12)
A James Bond movie that
includes a dramatic free-
running chase across a
construction site.

GoldenEye directed by
Martin Campbell (MGM,
1995; Certificate 12)
James Bond movie features
a spectacular bungee jump
in the opening scene.

Television

Extreme Sports Channel
Television channel devoted
to extreme sports, available
across Europe and the
Middle East.

Jump London directed by
Mike Christie (2003)
A television documentary
showing three free runners
performing near London
landmarks. A 2005 follow-
up by the same director
was called Jump Britain.

Websites

www.extreme.com/
Website of the Extreme
Sports Channel, which
has clips of sports action
and interviews with the
athletes involved.

**www.extremedreams.
co.uk/**
Website based around
the exploits of blind
extreme sports enthusiast
Dean Dunbar.

www.kidzworld.com/
Includes various pages
explaining the science
behind some extreme
sports.

**http://news.bbc.co.uk/
cbbcnews/**
A round-up of extreme
sports, with descriptions
and film footage.

www.youtube.com
Has amateur film action of
many extreme sports.

Index